GW00858901

Pinterest

A Book on Savvy Strategic Marketing of Your Business and How to Build a Following

By: Kaye Dennan

ISBN-13 978-1493502424

TABLE OF CONTENTS

PUBLISHERS NOTES

Disclaimer

Paperback Edition
Manufactured in the United States of America

DEDICATION

This book is dedicated to all online marketers who endeavor to spread the word about their business and help those who their business services.

WHAT IS PINTEREST?

Pinterest acts as a virtual pin board that helps you organize and share interests that you find on the web. As you surf, you can pin images from other sites onto Pinterest where others can re-pin those same images. This book is about how to maximize Pinterest for yur business since the new updates installed in Pinterest pre-October 2013.

WHY IS PINTEREST SO POPULAR?

The reason why Pinterest is so popular is because it is so easy to connect with others and build a community of like minded people. When Pinterest changed its format over several months from the beginning of 2013 there were some features that were improved but users complained that some of the features that made the use of Pinterest so popular had been taken away.

One very important statistic about Pinterest is the fact that it has a very strong following with women in the 30-49 age bracket who have disposable incomes and who, according to professional marketers, are believed to be the group of bigger spenders. This being the case, is Pinterest going to keep tweaking their site to cater to this angle of business? That we shall see over time.

The new features were Mentions and Pinned By which made it more difficult for them to connect with others. As I write this book some of the features are still being tweaked but Pinterest has taken notice of its users request and has installed or altered some of the new features to incorporate their desires.

Supposedly the bolder, cleaner look with the much bigger images (frames have been removed) is meant to encourage discovery. I do wonder how smaller screen users will react to these larger images over time.

Pinterest also lets you pin video from sites like Dailymotion, TED, YouTube and Vimeo using the Pin It button and as more pinners do this I think Pinterest will become even more popular.

Another popular feature of Pinterest is that by using the search features at the top left on the page you can easily search for more about your competitors by simply putting in their name or brand name to find out more. Or you may find them under a product name or keyword as well.

WHY SHOULD I USE PINTEREST?

Pinterest has become a social media site to be reckoned with. This quite simply is why you need to have a Pinterest account if you own a business. Initially people did not think that Pinterest was going to be a site from which you could make money but the opposite has proven to be the case.

Recent reports are saying that:

• Pinterest is now the third most popular social media site behind Facebook and Twitter

• Pinterest has amassed over 48.7 million users since its inception three years ago

• 69 of the world's top brands now using Pinterest and have discovered how to make money from it

• the best time to pin on Pinterest are 2pm -4pm and 8pm-1pm

• call to action pins see 80% increase in engagement

• tutorial and DIY pins enjoy over a 40% higher click through rate

Being an internet marketer myself, I am amazed how quickly I built up a following on Pinterest and how quickly I get results when I put up pins. When I started with Facebook I found it so difficult to build a list and there were so many rules and regulations that I seemed to always keep hitting a brick wall - I couldn't do this.....I couldn't do that...I could only have so many friends, etc., etc. None of that happens with Pinterest. It is so much easier to use.

Pinning is fun anyway, whether for business or whether you are just following your own personal interests, but when you are doing it for business then there are certain strategies that will get you far better results for all your effort.

As so many people do with Facebook and Twitter, you can have a business account and a personal account but because Pinterest is such visual concept many people don't seem to bother separating the two.

In saying that, if you are going to have the one account for both purposes then you do need to make that one account a business account because it is only when you have a business account that you can get the business benefits. We will be going through how to set up a business account further on.

One huge benefit I have seen with Pinterest is the fact that it is so visual. Not everyone can express themselves well with words so Pinterest allows them to find and pin pictures which show exactly what they were trying to express. This is such a help for those pinners.

Also because Pinterest is a visual concept people relate to it so much better, especially women. It is a known fact that we learn better if we can read and see concepts.

As a business person I find it fantastic because you communicate with more people in a much shorter time frame than you can on Facebook, Twitter, Google+ or Linkedin, which are the other four in the top five social media sites. I find that I can go into Pinterest a couple of times a day for 10-15 minutes, if that is all the time I have, and still get a good response.

Because you can so easily share a wide variety of your interests in such a short time you will find that you can soon collect a lot of followers of your various interests and they too will re-pin your pins. The sharing makes it so easy to get followers and you are not restricted as you are on some of the other sites. It is purely up to you if you want to follow someone, and followers cannot pin onto your boards unless you make them a group board and you invite them to do so.

The system easily shows you what people are re-pinning and it does give you a quick view of what others are finding appealing about your pins by using the analytics. A source that gives you feedback if you wish to maximize this strategy can be found at http://pinterest/source/YourWebsiteURL. Here you will be able to find out if your content is being pinned, what is being pinned and from that you will be able to pin more of the favorite topics to keep on attracting followers. You can get a fairly good idea by seeing what pinners are sharing and you can see this at the top right of your account.

Another excellent strategy that you can use Pinterest for is to do market research. It is so easy to find pins and boards on particular topics that you want information on. Not only that, once you have found those pins and boards you can easily be taken to the websites of these people where you can even further research information you may require. It is so simple to do this. All you have to do is go to the search box at the top left of the Pinterest page and type in a keyword or topic that you wish to research. You can then select whether you want to view boards or pins only and that will depend on how specific you want the search to be.

As you read through this book you will see that there are a number of strategies that you can implement to become a pinner to be reckoned with in your niche.

LET'S LOOK AT A PINTEREST ACCOUNT

Below are a series of screen shots to help you understand how Pinterest works.

Please refer to these images as you read through the book so that you understand and get the best from my instructions.

Image 1 – a set up account

This image shows your account as it would be when it is set up and you have clicked your account name to get the drop down box to appear.

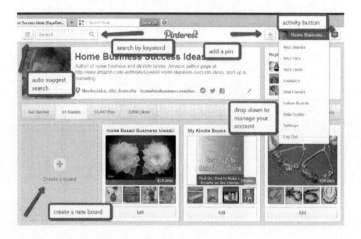

Image 2 – showing Secret Boards

In this image you will see how your secret boards are placed at the bottom of your account page. I have explained how to use secret boards for business purposes in 'Pinterest for business'.

Just as an aside in this image, you will see that the two boards just above the secret boards are group boards that I have joined – notice the large number of pins on those boards.

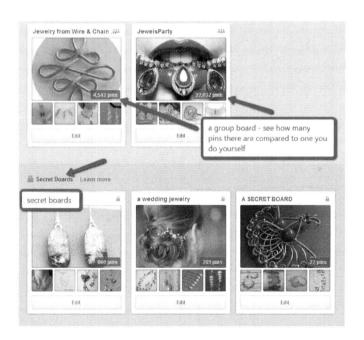

Image 3 – Showing finer account detail

With this image I wanted to point out the board titles (3) and how they are keyword related. The My Jewellery board is an interest board I have and it is a hobby based selling interest of mine. But if you notice the titles on the other boards, they are all related to either my websites or to ebooks I have written. Pinterest have now made the first board on your account a blank board that you can create as a new one (1). This is one of their new features.

It is important to have interesting pictures for your board cover (2) as other pinners will go through your boards to find out other boards that they may want to follow. Some pinners will click and follow all your boards, but other pinners will select certain boards to follow. To change the board cover just hover over the board and a box with the words 'Change Cover' on it will show, click on that and another popup will come up and all you need to do is scroll left or right for other pictures to view. Click your curser on the selected picture and slide it into the best position and hit save.

I think it is a good idea to change your cover every few months, but that is my personal choice with no stats to back it up.

Group boards (4) are shown by the 3 person cluster on the top right of your board. For my jewelry board I don't want others pinning to it so I have not set that up as a group board. But most of my others are but I have only invited several people per board at this stage.

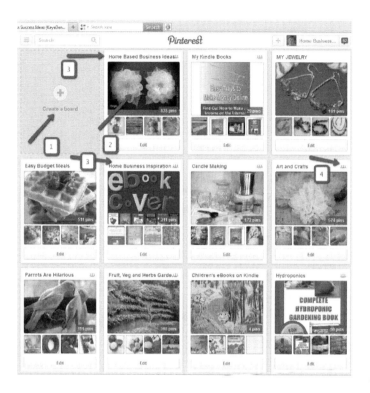

Image 4 – Enlarged Pin

When you click on an image as you are scrolling through Pinterest it will enlarge and there are several options there for you. At the bottom of the enlarged image Pinterest have added several other features. One is a row of other boards of like interest and if you click on the 'Show More' tag a whole range of other pins will appear. All this is to enable the pinner to find more and more pins of interest.

See Image 5 for more detail of what you can do from an enlarged pin. Numbers 1 – 6 apply to regular enlarged pins.

Image 5 - Pinterest Rich Pins (showing enlarged pin)

Although a new feature that the larger brands are embracing as time goes on, more and more small sellers will use Rich Pins as well. The screen shot below shows you a 'Rich Pin' that has been enlarged by clicking on the regular image. The enlarged image gives all the information for you as a buyer.

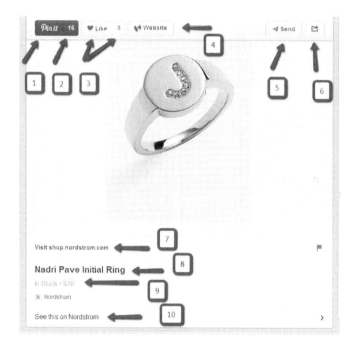

1.   Pin It button to repin

2.   The number of times it has already be repinned

3.   The Like button and the number indicates the number of times it has been liked already

4.   The link to the website

5.   Send button to send to a friend

6.   Send the image to an email address, Twitter or Facebook

7.   Essentially a 'buy button' without being a buy button

8.   The name of the item

9.   Information about whether it is in stock and the price

10.   Supplier name

What is the Difference When Pinning for Business

Remember, when you are pinning for business you obviously want to have a lot of pins about your business, but what you do need to remember is to keep a balance between your sales business pins and pins of interest.

Say for example, one of your passions is cooking and finding new recipes you will obviously be excited to pin these to a board or boards you have created. But if cooking does not in any way relate to your business then you don't want to bore your business followers with a whole lot of cooking recipes. But don't be concerned, it is easy to get around this. What you can do is have a 'secret board' and use that for storing all your favorite recipes that you see.

Say you are going through Pinterest and in a short space of time you find a lot of pins you want to share but do not want to bombard your followers with a bunch of the same pins, you can use a Secret board to store the extra pins and slow drip them out to your specific boards over a few days.

One of the ways to make sure that you do not lose followers is to make the effort to keep your business pins interesting. This is what I like about Pinterest. I can put up pictures that are interesting in themselves, but which relate to my business. If the pictures are interesting in themselves your followers will most likely not worry that you put up a few too many at one time.

SETTING UP YOUR PINTEREST BUSINESS ACCOUNT

1. Completing your profile

Start by setting up an account under your name. Use the email that you wish to have for the account or if you want to you can also sign up with your Facebook account.

Choose a name for your account. If you wish to have a business related name then you type this into your profile section.

Complete your profile section so that your followers will know what you are all about. Make sure that you put in your own website URL. Use a #hashtag in front of your keywords.

When you are using Pinterest for business there are a lot of extras that are available to you to help you promote your business so you want to make sure that you do set the account up to take advantage of these.

Upload a professional looking photo. If you feel you do not have one good enough try using Fiverr.com and see if anyone there can touch a photo up that you do have.

Take some time to put together something interesting for the 'About' section. This is an area where people will often visit to find out more about you.

As a final check, go over your account page and make sure all the settings are right. You need to make sure that the 'Search Privacy' setting is 'no' because you want your profile to be indexed by Google and for other search engines to find your content.

2. Add the 'Pin It' button to your browser

One of the features that Pinterest has is that you can add a 'Pin It' button to your browser and this makes the pinning of images so easy. At any time that you are using the computer and come across an image in a blog, a website, on Flickr, etc. all you have to do is click on the 'Pin It' button, it will bring up a selection of images from the open page and you can send your chosen image straight to your Pinterest account. You will be asked which board you want to pin it to, and presto, all done in a matter of seconds.

Here is the link where you can find upload the button to your browser: https://en.help.pinterest.com/entries/22997343-Add-the-Pin-It-button

3. Start creating your boards

Now that you have all the background work done all you have to do now is start creating some boards to attach your pins to. I love Pinterest, it is so easy to use and you have so much more control over your exposure than you do on other sites.

Why I say this is because if you set up a board that you no longer want, all you have to do is hit the 'edit' button and delete it. The same goes for a pin.

I mention this because when you are setting up your boards don't be too concerned about your choices. You can change your choices at any time that you wish simply by deleting them, or better still you can keep the board but change the board name and just delete pins from it that you no longer wish to have.

As this is a business account you will want to set up boards for that purpose so give some thought to the names of the boards so that when people are searching they will find your particular board. Try to work with keywords if you can. Many of the very popular keywords have been used so you may need to add some characters or such like so that you can use the name that you want: My Books might have to be My Own Books or Myy Books. You can also use adjectives to name your boards, like Colorful Parrots.

When you start set up about 10 boards, and as I say, you can add more or delete them as you wish. Although changing the boards too frequently would not be a good idea. It is not a good idea to have too wide a range of boards for the business account. By that I mean, say a personal interest of yours is fashion. It wouldn't be a good idea to have a whole range of boards in the account on fashion items: shoes, jewellery, pants, skirts, crop tops, sandals, hats, and so. That would just be too much and could overtake the purpose of having a business account. If you do want to have loads of boards on a particular topic that is not your business then it's best to set up a personal account for items of that number.

When you set up your new board edit the board and add a description to it and also add a link to your website, your book or whatever it is that you are doing for business. Write it so that the reader will understand exactly why you set the board up.

4. Pinning

The purpose of pinning is to attract people of like interest to your boards and to do this you need to pin selectively and pin good quality content. So many of the pins that do get uploaded do not have any description to them at all and quite frankly unless the image is absolutely stunning you want to avoid those pins because they have no purpose. If the pins are not attractive people do not share them anyway and let's face it that is the ultimate purpose.

It is a matter of quality not quantity.

Creating a new board when pinning: when pinning you may come across an image which inspires you to create another board and this is easy enough to do. When you have clicked the pin button a pop up box will ask you which board you want to pin to. Just click on the drop down box for your boards and you will see that it asks you if you want to create a new board. Click on that and create your board, but don't forget to go back and edit in the relevant details of that new board from your own account page.

Working with and sharing pins: if you hover over a pin you will be able to use the Pin It button or the Like button. You can click the Like button twice to Unlike an image if you change your mind. If you click on the Pin It button a popup box will show and you can then select which board you want to send the pin to. Notice also the boxes on the bottom left of the popup box to allow you to share on Twitter.

The Comment feature that had an icon on the front has gone from that position and is now on the enlarged image once you have clicked on the picture. Also on the enlarged image is the Send button if want to send the pin to a friend or to Twitter or Facebook. View these on Image 5 above. Again, on this new Pinterest setup, the enlarged image has at the top an icon of the world and if you want to follow through to a website click on that and it will take you through to it.

There are several ways to add pins to your boards:

Uploading from your computer: it is very easy to upload a pin from your computer simply by going to the top of the page in your Pinterest account and clicking on the + button then click on 'Upload Pin' then browse through you computer. What is so good about this is that you will be choosing images that you have pre-selected or they most likely would not have been kept by you in the first place.

Adding from a website: go again to the + at the top of the page and click on 'Add from a Website'. All you have to do here is add in the image location from another website and it will bring up the image for you to pin to one of your boards. Alternatively if you have added the 'Pin It' button to your browser you can do it that way.

Making up your own pin: a popular system for business pinners is to create an image of their own. These may be in the form of an infographic, a topical image which someone has put together or a run of images that show how something is made. These learning pins or tutorial pins are great as long as they are done well. The best way is to have the top image a photo of the completed piece and then follow on with the instruction images for making the item. I have a lot of these in my board for home business ideas and you can view them here:

http://www.pinterest.com/KayeDennan/home-based-business-ideas/

You will see how some are as I mentioned and others start with the making of the item and some don't even have the completed item picture. The reason that you want to put the finished item first is because that is what people see when they are scrolling through looking for pins to share and a good picture tweaks their interest.

If you are building your own images then keep in mind that they are best if they are about 530 x 800 or just slightly bigger. Tall images are best as they run down the page and the viewer's attention is attracted to them as they scroll down the page.

Another type of pin that you might like to upload is a quote. I use Quozio.com which is so easy, not the fanciest, but it does the job well and I do get a good response with well thought out quotes. You just build your quote in Quozio and from their you can send it straight to Pinterest. You can send to Facebook and Twitter as well.

Adding links: if you are pinning from your blog onto Pinterest then you shouldn't have to add a link back to your website because it has been embedded into the graphic and when the viewer clicks on it they will be able to access that link. But the reality is that not everyone knows to do this so if you do want them to click through to your blog or somewhere else, add that link to your description. This is the best way to ensure that they will know what to do. Even better still say: "click this link" and they will know exactly what to do.

Protecting your own built images: when you have taken the time to build an image you don't want to have the link to it lost, as sometimes does happen in all the sharing that goes on. The best way to do this is to Watermark your image with your name and your URL. It is the surest and best way to protect your work. There are a number of tools for photo editing such as: PicMonkey, MorgueFile, Phonto App, Instagram and Snapseed. Check them out and find one that you can easily use.

Sharing written content: let's say you have some written content that you have found that you want to share with your fellow Pinners but it has no image so you cannot just hit the 'Pin It' button and add it. All you have to do is find a relevant image, probably from your computer, pin it and then make sure that the description gives the link to where you want them to go to read the content.

Using the Secret board: 'Secret' boards have several purposes and I have explained further on how it can be used specifically for business, but they also have a purpose for managing your pin sharing. As you are searching for pins to share you may come across a board that has a lot of pins you want to repin. This is great but if you re-in them all at once you may lose followers who do not particularly want to see those pins so the idea is to create a Secret board as in Image 2 and put the excess pins in there then at a later date you drip feed them out to your named boards.

BUILDING A COMMUNITY

Quite simply it comes down to the fact that the more people you follow the more you are going to have good pins to share. Pinterest does have a fantastic system for following. Each time you share a pin there is a pop up box which appears and which makes the suggestion that you follow. What you will find is that anyone who is shown in this box is not someone that you are already following. If the board appeals to you then it is really easy to just hit the 'follow' button. If the graphics are really interesting then you may want to right click the pop up box and get it to open up in a new window. This way you can look through all the boards that that particular person has without losing your place in your work.

It is very easy to get followers as long as you are pinning quality and interesting pins. With a business account you do need to make sure that the majority of your pins relate to your business or would have an appeal to your followers.

Expand your reach from your blog

As mentioned before if you add the 'Pin It' button to your browser you will be able to grab images from almost any website or page where you see something that is applicable. At this point in time Facebook and Pinterest are not sharing friendly as regards using the Pin It button, but what you can do is make a jpeg of an image with Jing (a free downloadable tool from the internet), save the file to your computer and then you can upload it to the other site. It doesn't take long to do this and it works a treat.

Put a Pinterest widget on your blog

This is a great idea. You can put a widget on your blog and it will bring up images from a specific board that you have. Just go to http://tinyurl.com/mknm7xq and you will be able to set it up. From this same page you add a Pin hover button to your site as well. You can see the Pinterest widget on my website at: http://homebusnesssuccessideas.com. I have had a lot of success with this strategy.

Get to know your Community

So that you can get the best from your Pinterest account you need to observe where your pins are being shared to, in other words what the names are of the boards the pins are going to. What sort of board are they being shared on.

Are your followers 'getting you'?

In other words, are you reaching your ideal client with the pins that you are putting up or are they not on the same wave length as you. For example if you put up a pin as an inspirational quote, you don't want people pinning it to their 'funny' board.

Get on to Group Boards

There is a type of board that you can get on called a 'Group Board'. You can set these up yourself and invite pinners or you can go out and seek these boards and ask for an invite. The board is just a normal board but the creator of the board has set it up in such a way that other pinners can be invited to pin on it. The idea is that these boards will often have several thousand pinners belonging to them so when you pin on them your pin is reaching far and wide. They are a great way to get known really fast. If you set up your own, do some research and invite people with like interest to pin to the board and you will see it grows really fast. Unfortunately a lot of pinners do not understand the benefit of these boards and do not reply back and join in when you send out invites. As time goes on more and more people will be in their group boards.

If you get invited to join a Group Board do make sure that It fits in with your goals or you could be wasting a lot of time. There will be plenty around with like interests to you.

A BUSINESS FEATURE

Earlier in the book I referred to the use of Secret boards and the obvious is to use them for keeping pins that you don't want to share with others or to store pins to share at a later date.

In Image 2 above you will see that I have 3 secret boards and I use these to collect ideas for my jewelry hobby.

A collaborative Secret board

An excellent use of a secret board for business is to use it as a collaborative board for several staffers to use, much like Evernote and the like.

You can have a group of workers who can access the business account and who can then access the Secret boards. It means that you can share ideas, pins, even script if you wish, share private messages and the like. This way you can keep all this information private and only pin out of the secret board anything you want to share.

Planning a Promotion

Another idea is that you could set up a Secret board for a future promotion. You put all your pins into the Secret board and then when the promotion begins you can share them out of there into the community as and when you want. This really helps with your pre-organization when promoting products, books, courses or anything you have coming out.

MAKING MONEY FROM PINTEREST

It's not possible to sell directly on Pinterest as you might on Etsy or eBay for example, but it is possible to get people to buy from you because they saw your pin.

A feature on the upgraded Pinterest is called Rich Pins and already this has been embraced by the large merchants to sell their products through Pinterest.

Rich Pins

There are 3 types of rich pins available: products, recipes and movies.

These pins provide more information about their topic image so a pinner can now buy right from the page.

To use a Rich Pin you do have to have it approved by Pinterest first. There are certain requirements so to read through all the requirements click on your account button on the top right, go to help and write into the search box ' rich pins' and there you will see all the information you will need. Because this is a new feature and is believed to be one that will become very popular I have not written instructions here because as Pinterest upgrade it I believe any instructions here will change sooner rather than later.

Also when you have a business account you can put a price with a dollar sign in your description and it will automatically carry across to a price bar on the image. This will work on your regular pins when you put a price in the description but also in the Rich Pins.

Rich Pins are a way to send targeted buys directly to your products for sale. Once you are set up for this method you can convert your already existing pins to Rich Pins provided the meta tag information has been added to the source page.

Make Sales through an Optin Box

What you can do which works well is have interesting graphics that ask pinners to go to a certain opt-in box through the link to down load something like a FREE report, or some other giveaway that you will use to get names for your database.

Once you have these names then you can market to them and sell them from there. You can add a 'click here' tag to anything you pin about your business to get viewers to go through to your site.

Alternatively you can link straight through to your products.

Other ways to Make Money from Pinterest:

• You can pin a discount on products, pin your promotions, your ebooks or instruction manuals.

- If you are launching a book or a new product you can market it on your boards.

- You can even get people to follow through to your website and enter to win a prize by opting in to a competition. Of course, you will need to make the prize attractive to get people to opt in and fit within certain guidelines for competitions.

PINTEREST ANALYTICS

To get an idea at a glance of who is pinning your content and what is proving to be your most popular content, start using the Pinterest Analytics tool. Go to the top of your page, click on the box at the top and in the drop down box click on Analytics.

PLUGINS

When you upload plugins make sure that you edit the settings so that it works to your desired purposes.

Pinterest Follow button

http://wordpress.org/plugins/pinterest-follow-button/

this plugin will add a widget to your side bar. A must to get followers.

Pinterest Pinboard Widget

http://wordpress.org/plugins/pinterest-pinboard-widget/

if you have a product website this is a must. The widget ads a box to the sidebar of your website and the pictures change as you upload pins to the board you select. I have used this and had a huge success with it.

"Pin It " button

http://wordpress.org/plugins/pinterest-pin-it-button/

using this plugin means that you only have to add this plugin to your site and then you no longer have to add codes to each page or post.

"Pin Button Attraction"

http://pinbuttonattraction.com/?aff=19432

this is a premium button which means you do have to purchase it. When you have loaded it up a little red PIN box sites on your images in the top left corner. The cost at the time of publication is $19.97. It is a very good way to entice your viewers to pin your graphics and ultimately your URL.

Pinterest Lightbox

http://wordpress.org/plugins/pinterest-lightbox/

this plugin automatically enables a "Pin It" button on each image through your NextGEN Gallery.

Pinterest Block

http://wordpress.org/plugins/pinterest-block/

maybe you won't have the need for this plugin, but if you do then you can access it here. There may be content that you don't want shared through Pinterest and this is the way to do it.

PINTEREST TOOLS

Free Tools

1.   Pixlr.com – a photo editing tool for those who do not have Photoshop

2.   Piktochart – allows you to create your own infographics which are very popular

3.   Pinerly – as long as you pin the image through Pinerly first you can get stats of your pins such as repins, click throughs and more

4.   Picmarkr – you can add a watermark, copyright and logo to your images

5.   Pingraphy – you can schedule your pins with this tool

6.   Pinstamastic – this will help you really jazz up your images, quotes and also create images from visited websites and more

7.   Ipiccy – a photo editing tool

NEW ADDITION TO PINTEREST JULY 2015

E-commerce has become an integral part of all businesses irrespective of their location. A good networking and promotion of products and services can do great wonders. To be able to benefit its users, Pinterest has launched several new features as a part of constant evolution. Pinterest has structured a simple guided procedure for you or your web developer to tag along for capitalizing your businesses opportunities. In order to begin, there are a few Meta tags that would be required to be added to your business website before a subsequent approval process. Upon approval, Pinterest would mechanically collect relevant information whenever you or a consumer pins from it.

However, these features may appear to be a U-turn from the original features at first. Nevertheless, they do have their pros and cons as and when applied. In addition to this, some of the existing features were re-modeled to be able to engage and benefit its users. Enlisted below are the new additions to Pinterest:

Buy It

The latest addition to the Pinterest is the **buyable Pins** that facilitate a simple, secure way to buy your favorite products on Pinterest. Currently, this service is rolled out to its U.S. Pinners over iPhone and iPad. It works on a simple mechanism that is loved by everyone. When the **Buy It** button is blue that means you can buy. The price of the product featured would appear in blue and that indicates its availability to buy. For instance, you are looking for a dining table all you need to do is search for the desired item. Once you get the list of available options, just swipe through the buyable pins. The good part is that you can filter by the price before deciding upon the right item for yourself. This is not all; you can compare the color choices by means of this pin too. In case, you aren't planning to buy yet, then simply Pin It, and come back later to buy it.

This pin revolutionizes the new ways to shop, taking e-commerce to the next level. To get the latest products on Pinterest, browse through the Shop category and you would find a wide range of options to choose from.

Users using the Pinterest app on their phone can easily confirm a purchase by tapping on the Buy It tab. The users can make a payment by using Apple Pay or Credit Card. For the ease of the users, the personal information submitted for payment is saved to its confidential database for future use. With these simple clicks, you can have your favorite product shipped to you. It is assumed that about *30 million Pins* would have buyable tabs in the coming weeks. Some of the popular brands such as Gardener's Supply Company, Macy and many Shopify stores are expected to feature on Pinterest with this new Pin.

In order to view pins from a specific store, you would simply need to search for their Pinterest profile that feature all their latest products with **Buy It** pins. This feature can be availed on iPhone and iPad *but only in the US for now.* Pinterest does promise a worldwide launch of this new buyable pin sometime soon, until then those outside the US have to wait. Nevertheless, the overwhelming response of users to this new pin anticipates the possibility that it won't be long before you will find several blue **Buy It** buttons all across Pinterest. This service is definitely going to make shopping much more fun and easy.

Promoted Pins

The name of the pin in itself is suggestive that it promotes local or area businesses through "call-for-action" or images that scream out. With business realizing the power of this latest technology, more and more businesses in the US are paying Pinterest for promotion as well as visibility. The prime aim of these pins is to promote niche businesses and expose them to a larger audience.

These Promoted Pins are basically *paid Pins* by businesses to reach out to their targeted clientele. It is likely that you may have relevant **Promoted Pins** displayed on your page in accordance to your indicated interests and pinning activity on Pinterest. These pins are quite different from the 'Picked for You' Pins. The handpicked pins are usually based upon your personal interests whereas **Promoted Pins** are paid for promoting third parties (affiliate products) or businesses.

Promoted Pins are a good opportunity to get an exposure in the market without much hard work. These pins create a pool of audience that can be a potential loyal clientele leading to a successful marketing campaign.

Related Boards

The related boards feature is a great way to see that might interest you. One can be pinning new content that can be shared with your followers or simply following other boards that may catch your interest. These two pinning exercises work absolutely parallel to each other. These related boards appear as options that you may like to browse while taking a look at your specific search on Pinterest. This feature can be availed through the mobile app, with a simple tap on the cover of any given board and hold. After this, you just need to slide your finger towards the light bulb icon and release enabling lists of boards that have similar or related pins and titles.

This is definitely a great way to find new boards as well as follow boards of specific or same interest. It allows you to connect with our people who share your interest of marketing. It is an easy way to look out for new avenues for your business. In addition to this, a look at related boards can give you insight into what type of boards people are pinning your content to as well as it could act as an inspiration for new content or new products for your business. In short, it serves as a catalyst for businesses to shape ideas to improve and create products and services in accordance to the market trends.

Notifications

Pinterest has come up with an interesting way to keep you updated through its notification feature. The **Notifications** service is fairly old but it is constantly updated to meet the challenges of the market. Earlier the notifications primarily indicated repins from your boards. However, the new version of this service keeps you updated about even a tiny collage of the boards, and sometimes showing the entire board. Although it does sound that much damage has been done to the existing service but it isn't so. Although, the past service allowed you to take a glance at all the activities in one go but the new version gives you a more detailed take on the activity. In fact, it might seem like a nuisance with notifications about re-pins, followers and much more but it definitely keeps you updated. This feature allows you to look at your Pinterest account with regard to who has been following it or the number of likes for a specific board. This gives you the opportunity to see where you may need to add new products to your list due to interest or alternatively see where a product you have is not getting the interest that you thought it would

The notifications change is applicable to both the web as well as mobile Pinterest versions, so that you can make the most of it.

News

The news services on Pinterest works on the similar lines of Notifications. However, unlike notifying about your boards or pins, this feature informs about the pins made by others. Inspiration is definitely a good way to get creative ideas for your businesses. This service allows you to see pins or boards created by your followers or the ones you follow that widens your scope of pinning some of the interesting and related pins. The **News** feature alerts you as well as keeps you on track with the possible pins that you may like to pin sharing different interests with friends' and followers. It could actually work quite well to generate traffic and sales to your website as you would be well-acquainted with the probable strategies and trends applied by your competitors. Although it does sound extremely simple and basic it is a powerful tool that can revamp or widen your business ideas for better prospects.

Pinterest is likely to come up with more benefitting and interesting features as it evolves that may accentuate your business opportunities. It is extremely important to tap into these opportunities as they act as online marketing tools without the elaborate procedure. If these are used in an appropriate and guided manner, these features or services can be magical for your business, a blessing in disguise.

Once you start using Pinterest for your business, you may not prefer anything more or above it. It is crucial to be updated every now and then about its latest features or services so that you are always at the edge of the market trends and a step ahead of competitors. Pinterest is a powerful marketing tool that is affordable and easy to handle without complications. One can simply continue to manage their business accounts on Pinterest along with customizing to its latest features.

Make the best use of these latest features and services on Pinterest and stay tuned for many more in the future. Happy Pinning!

PS: I have tried to keep you abreast of the changes as I believe Pinterest is a wonderful marketing tool, especially for those customers that like visual connection. What is so good about Pinterest is that the pins are kept and available unless they are manually removed, as opposed to Facebook or Twitter where it is not so easy to find graphics of a particular interest very easily.

This easy to use tool can be quite time consuming, as is nearly all the social media tools, so limit your time for business and personal use so that you do not neglect your business.   When I first started using Pinterest several years ago I was in awe of the pictures covering interests that I have. I hope you too enjoy it as much as I have over the years.

CONCLUSION

When using Pinterest for business ensure sure that it is working for you, not against you. Only pin what you are happy to share and share only what you want your perceived client base to understand about you.

Have fun and enjoy the wonderful pins that are on Pinterest.

ABOUT THE AUTHOR

Kaye Dennan has been an internet marketer for over 7 years and during that time has used a large number of the social media sites to promote her various websites.

Kaye started out with very little knowledge of internet marketing and like so many others has had to learn the hard way. What has excited her so much is the success that she has been having on Pinterest.com to the point that most of her contacts actually come from Pinterest now.

With over 30 years in small business behind her Kaye, who bought her first business in her early 20's, has shared a lot of her business skills, experience, both good and bad, tips and marketing skills on her website HomeBusinessSuccessIdeas.com. It is with this experience behind her that Kaye does not lead people into believing that owning a business is easy, because it is not. It is full of challenges, but when you love what you are doing, as she does, you will embrace those challenges and keep surging forward with your goals.

ADULT WORD SEARCH VOLUME 1

https://www.createspace.com/5020196

ADULT WORD SEARCH VOLUME 2

https://www.createspace.com/5021897

KIDS WORD SEARCH VOL 1

https://www.createspace.com/5002002

KIDS WORD SEARCH VOL 2

https://www.createspace.com/5004213

Over 80 Other Books By

Kaye Dennan

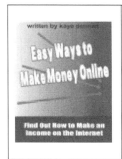  

Available From Her

Amazon Author Page

http://www.amazon.com/-/e/B00AVQ6KKM

Pinterest

http://pinterest.com/KayeDennan

17550648R00032

Printed in Great Britain
by Amazon